REAL HISTORY!
Massive Disasters

Amazing But True Stories of America and Its Heros

REAL HISTORY!

Puzzles, Fun Facts, and More!

Massive Disasters

EDWARD N. PERKINS

Illustrated by TOM LYNCH

Applewood Books
Carlisle, Massachusetts

Massive Disasters
The REAL History Series

All original source material included in this book is reproduced
accurately with spelling and grammatical errors intact.

Copyright ©2020 Applewood Books, Inc.

All rights reserved. No part of this book may be
reproduced in any form or by any electronic or
mechanical means without permission in
writing from the publisher, except by a
reviewer who may quote brief
passages in a review.

ISBN: 978-1-4290-9544-0

All illustrations by Tom Lynch.

Published by
Applewood Books
Carlisle, Massachusetts 01741
To request a free copy of our current catalog
featuring our best-selling books, write to:
Applewood Books, Inc.
P.O. Box 27
Carlisle, Massachusetts 01741

www.awb.com

CONTENTS

October 10, 1780 The Great Hurricane Devastates the Caribbean — **1**

December 16, 1811 The New Madrid Earthquake Roils Missouri — **9**

March 29, 1848 Niagara Falls Runs Dry — **17**

August 28, 1859 A Massive Solar Storm (The Carrington Event) Hits the Earth — **25**

October 8, 1871 The Midwest Goes Up in Flames — **35**

August 21, 1883 The Mayo Clinic is Conceived in an F5 Tornado — **43**

March 12, 1888 The Blizzard of '88 — **51**

May 31, 1889 The Great Johnstown Flood — **59**

March 25, 1911 The Triangle Shirtwaist Fire — **67**

June 22, 1918 The Hammond Circus Train Disaster — **75**

September 2, 1935 Great Labor Day Hurricane Hits the Florida Keys — **83**

August 18, 1961 "The Birds" Invade Santa Cruz — **93**

OCTOBER 10, 1780

The Great Hurricane Devastates the Caribbean

By the fall of 1780, the American Revolution was winding down. The British and French navies were jousting with each other to determine who would control the rich colonies of the West Indies. The British controlled the island of Barbados. It hadn't been hit by a hurricane for over 100 years. Nobody was overly concerned as dawn broke that morning of October 10, and gale force winds started rushing in from the northwest.

Soon the rain and wind increased to hur-

ricane force. By nine o'clock that evening it reached such a fury that its force was stripping not just the leaves, but the very bark off the trees as well. That means the winds must have exceeded 200 miles per hour. The storm raged savagely until early the next morning. By daybreak every public building, including the castle, the forts, and the church, and almost every house in Bridgetown were leveled to the ground.

The British had a fleet of twelve warships patrolling the Caribbean. Eight of the warships sank in the St. Lucia harbor that day. Hundreds of sailors drowned. The stone forts and military barracks on St. Lucia were destroyed. Heavy cannons were carried hundreds of feet off their positions. Only two houses were left standing, and more than six thousand persons perished on the island.

The French

fared even worse. As the hurricane bore down on Martinique, it enveloped a convoy of French transports and sunk more than forty ships carrying 4,000 soldiers. The island itself was no refuge. Nine thousand people died from a huge storm surge.

At St. Vincent, every building was blown down and the capital, Kingstown destroyed. At Grenada, nineteen Dutch ships were stranded and bashed to pieces. On St. Pierre, every house was blown down. More than 1,000 people perished. Five thousand lives were lost on St. Eustatius. The storm hit virtually every island from Tobago in the southeast through the Leeward Islands across to Hispaniola, from Barbados, where neither trees nor dwellings were left standing, to Dominique, St. Eustatius, St. Vincent, and Puerto Rico. Any vessel in the path of the cyclone foundered with all their crews.

Beyond Puerto Rico, the tempest bent toward the Bermudas, where it gradually diminished. But still it sunk several English warships returning to Europe as it passed over the Atlantic shipping lanes.

The Great Hurricane of 1780 was the most destructive hurricane ever recorded in the Caribbean. Over 22,000 people died. Beyond the toll in human suffering, the storm dealt a powerful blow to both British and French colonial aspirations in the western hemisphere. It also cleared the path for the growth of the fragile young American republic.

Thought Question

Today we have technology to make fairly accurate predictions about hurricanes and tropical storm activity. Why do you think storms can still have such a huge impact on human lives and property?

_____

_____

_____

_____

_____

_____

FASCINATING 5 FACTS
YOU MAY NOT KNOW

1. The 1780 hurricane season was the worst in recorded history, with about 27,000 people dead.

2. In the 18th century, most residents of the Caribbean just looked at the sky to predict bad storms, but ships tried to schedule travel around the hurricane season.

3. Because no one kept detailed storm records back in 1780, wind speeds are estimated based on eyewitness accounts (e.g., trees were stripped of bark, indicating wind speeds of over 200 miles per hour).

4. Modern-day ships move fast enough to get out of the way of a hurricane, but back then there were few options if you were at sea.

5. Florida gets hit by more hurricanes than any other U.S. state, but China gets hit more often than any other country in the world (though they call the storms typhoons)!

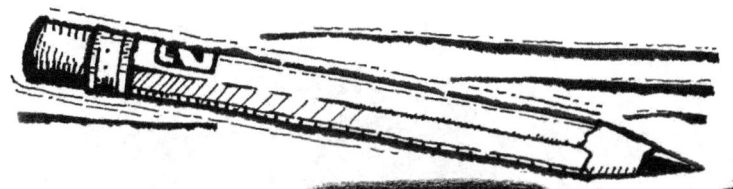

WORD SEARCH

```
T D M Z N A E B B I R A C N E
D U H A Q M N O I G Y H L W W
G S C U R A A H T W S E F B H
L Y G A Z T C U K E D Y H A N
A G A J B N I B S H I P S M E
M F M E E A R N S R G N I W U
T Y P R L A R B I R R B T W K
Q B F C R R U B I Q Y I I Q I
I U I K O P H W A W U N R H F
I Q P M N Z D I J D D E B C R
S G F N B G C R E S O Y C V N
S Y L T K U E S Y O Q S J U W
R L X Y L S E I N O L O C D O
H K K T I F M W P P F V B F R
O I S R N O I T U L O V E R D
```

BARBADOS
COLONIES
HURRICANE
SHIPS
BRITISH
DROWN
MARTINIQUE
ST. LUCIA
CARIBBEAN
FRENCH
REVOLUTION
WINDS

DECEMBER 16, 1811

The New Madrid Earthquake Roils Missouri

On the 16th of December, 1811, about two o'clock, A.M., we were visited by a violent shock of an earthquake, accompanied by a very awful noise resembling loud but distant thunder, but more hoarse and vibrating, which was followed in a few minutes by the complete saturation of the atmosphere, with sulphurious [sic] vapor, causing total darkness. The screams of the affrighted inhabitants running to and fro, not knowing where to go, or what to do—the cries of the fowls and beasts of every species—the cracking of trees falling, and the roaring of the Mississippi—the current of which was retrograde for a few minutes, owing as is supposed, 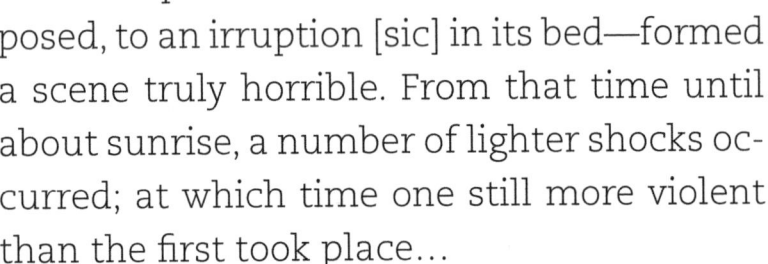 to an irruption [sic] in its bed—formed a scene truly horrible. From that time until about sunrise, a number of lighter shocks occurred; at which time one still more violent than the first took place...

The inhabitants fled in every direction to the country, supposing (if it can be admitted that their minds were exercised at all) that there was less danger at a distance from, than near to the river. In one person, a female, the alarm was so great that she fainted, and could not be recovered...

At first the Mississippi seemed to recede from its banks, and its waters gathering up like a mountain, leaving for a moment many boats, which were here on their way to

New Orleans, on the bare sand, in which time the poor sailors made their escape from them. It then rising fifteen to twenty feet perpendicularly, and expanding, as it were, at the same moment, the banks were overflowed with a retrograde current, rapid as a torrent—the boats which before had been left on the sand were now torn from their moorings, and suddenly driven up a little creek, at the mouth of which they laid, to the distance in some instances, of nearly a quarter of a mile. The river falling immediately, as rapid as it had risen, receded in its banks again with such violence, that it took with it whole groves of young cotton-wood trees, which ledged its borders...

A great many fish were left on the banks, being unable to keep pace with the water. The river was literally covered with the wrecks of boats, and 'tis said that one was wrecked in which there was a lady and six children, all of whom were lost. In all the hard shocks mentioned, the earth was horribly torn to pieces...

We were constrained by the fear of our houses falling to live twelve or eighteen months, after the first shocks, in little light camps made of boards; but we gradually became callous, and returned to our houses again...

I have now, sir, finished my promised description of the earthquake—imperfect it is true, but just as it occurred to my memory; many of, and most of the truly awful scenes, having occurred three or four years ago...

Your humble servant,
Eliza Bryan

A written account sent from Eliza Bryan to Lorenzo Dow in 1816.

Thought Question

Have you ever experienced a destructive natural disaster? Why do you think people choose to remain in areas where there is a higher likelihood of natural disasters, like earthquakes?

_____

_____

_____

_____

_____

_____

5 FASCINATING FACTS YOU MAY NOT KNOW

1. According to some reports, the 1811 earthquake was so strong that it caused church bells to ring 1,000 miles away, in Boston, Massachusetts.

2. Because of the December 16 earthquake, the Mississippi River actually flowed backward for several hours.

3. Other strange things happened after the earthquake, like sand boils (small springs that pop up in sand) and seismoluminescence (lights that come up from the ground).

4. Hundreds of schools in and around Missouri were closed on December 3, 1990 because a scientist had predicted another big earthquake on that day, but nothing happened.

5. There is no proven way to predict where and when an earthquake will happen.

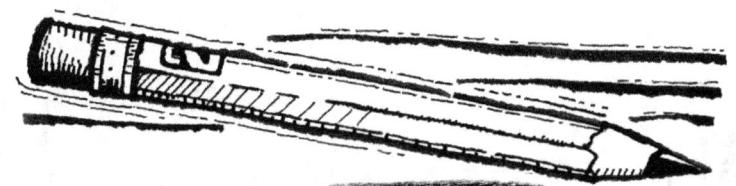

WORD SEARCH

```
P I X L B Z N U Q T J K C A X
R Z Y M I B E P X H I E D X E
E O O X I V W A Y U B H S Z C
D F Y O P A M S G N G R I N M
I D N E F P A O N D F C R I D
C Z B L A O D G M E F R U N C
T M F Q X R R G P R I J O U Y
I P P I S S I S S I M N S P I
K O O P C X D A R K N E S S Q
D S Q S H A K I N G N Z I M O
E K A U Q H T R A E V K M Z F
G S S N D R N W H Z C L M P I
T G V B D S V D I A N Y M K S
V D C G C L Z Y Y R O R R E T
P W P G C U R R E N T L U F F
```

CURRENT	DARKNESS	EARTHQUAKE
MISSISSIPPI	MISSOURI	NEW MADRID
PREDICT	SAND	SHAKING
TERROR	THUNDER	VAPOR

MARCH 29, 1848

Niagara Falls Runs Dry

Jed Porter farmed the fields along the Niagara River just upstream from Niagara Falls. Late in the evening of March 29, 1848, he stepped outside to take in the night air. He suddenly realized that something was strangely amiss. There was a silence he had never heard before. The thundering roar of the Falls was missing!

When his neighbors woke up the next morning, the eerie silence and the missing mist from the falls drew them to the river's shore. There they discovered that the water flow of the Niagara River had been reduced to a mere trickle. When the first employees arrived at the water-powered Bridgewater Mills they found the mill race was empty, and the mill had to be shut down.

Word spread quickly. The riverbed was quickly drying. Fish and turtles were left floundering on now dry land. A number of people made their way into the gorge to the riverbed. They picked up articles that had been laying hidden on the river's bottom for years. They found bayonets, gun barrels, muskets, tomahawks, and other artifacts of the War of 1812.

By the morning of March 31, more than 5,000 people had gathered along the banks of the river. Men were able to walk out onto the riverbed that had only hours earlier been a torrent of rapids. A squad of soldiers of the U.S. Army Cavalry rode their horses up and down

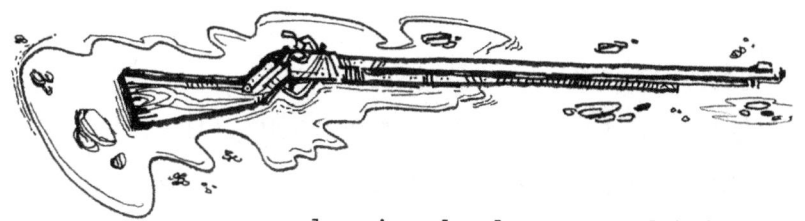

the riverbed as an exhibition.

The sudden silencing of the roar of the Falls was strange. Some believed that this event signaled the beginning of the end of the world. Thousands of people filled the churches and prayed for the falls to start flowing and the world to continue. Or they prayed for salvation and forgiveness of their sins as the Last Judgment approached. No one knew why the falls had stopped.

Then news arrived from Buffalo that strong southwest gale winds had pushed huge chunks of lake ice to the extreme northeastern tip of Lake Erie. This blocked the lake's outlet into the head of the Niagara River. The ice jam had become an ice dam.

On the night of March 31, 1848, the wind shifted. The ice dam at the mouth of the Niagara River at Lake Erie broke apart. A loud low-pitched growl and groan was heard coming from upstream. A wall of water rushed forward at surprising speed, filled the river, and surged over the falls. The ice jam cleared, and the river was running again. The residents along the river rejoiced at the return of the roar of the falls.

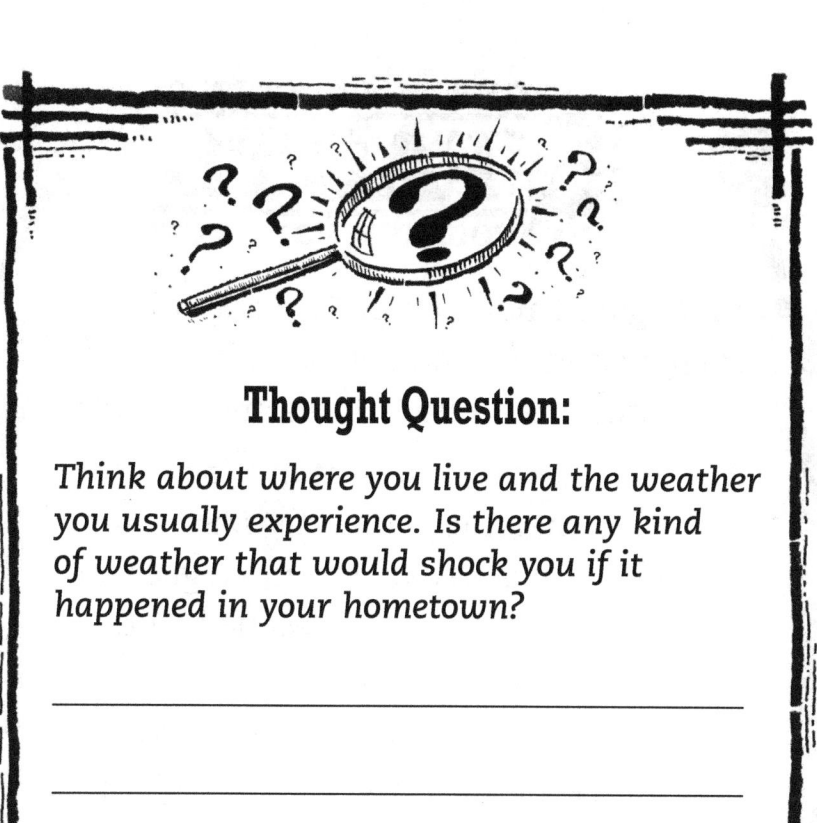

Thought Question:

Think about where you live and the weather you usually experience. Is there any kind of weather that would shock you if it happened in your hometown?

_____

_____

_____

_____

_____

_____

_____

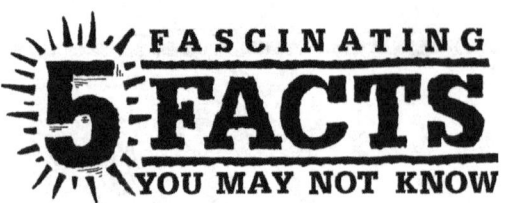

5 FASCINATING FACTS YOU MAY NOT KNOW

1. Niagara Falls is actually made up of three waterfalls and cuts across two countries: the United States and Canada.

2. The biggest tourist boat at Niagara Falls is named the *Maid of the Mist*, after a legend about a Native American girl who goes over the falls and is rescued by the gods.

3. People have tried to ride down Niagara Falls in wooden and steel barrels, giant rubber balls, inner tubes, and even a jet ski.

4. Hundreds of people have died at Niagara Falls, including many suicides, a handful of daredevils, and a bunch of animals who were unwillingly sent over in a publicity stunt.

5. Only eleven people have survived going over the falls, including Annie Edson Taylor, a 62-year-old teacher.

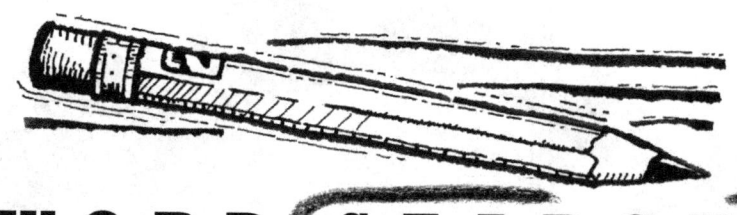

WORD SEARCH

```
L Y Q T Q D M F A S B O V H V
Y Z L I C G M K S Y N G B M O
K O X C K S E M Y V H U E M Z
Z S M E A D N E G E L A K F R
M F R O L O L W V L F L T T C
O I D H S G D H O H L R I A Z
E O L S D B O D C A N A D A Z
F T Y E C I G R F A A W V I W
R S R S J Q A R I C F R L J Z
V I J R J D E M Z V K L L D N
I M K O Y T P R I L E U G N N
W B P H A R A G A I N R U P P
U Z N W K C D Y Y L B W B L D
J W Y B N A C I R E M A Y E C
P M U R Z G H Z F K G T W L D
```

AMERICAN	CANADA	DRY
ERIE	HORSESHOE	ICE
LEGEND	MAID	MIST
NIAGARA	RIVERBED	WATERFALL

AUGUST 28, 1859

A Massive Solar Storm (The Carrington Event) Hits the Earth

On August 28, 1859, astronomers first noticed the appearance of an uncommonly large number of sunspots on the sun. The next night, large displays of the aurora borealis lit up the night skies around the world. On September 1, astronomers Richard C. Carrington and Richard Hodgson observed, for the first time, a solar flare flashing from the surface of the sun.

Something strange was going on. One of the largest solar storms ever recorded was happening. It was disrupting the geomagnetic fields of Earth.

The Boston Transcript reported that in Vermont *"at seven and a half o'clock, we were notified of a large fire behind the mountain at the* north, and we went out to see it: and presently the red clouds began to disappear, and spires of green shot up from the same place. It was the most magnificent display ever witnessed in this section; the sky for about an hour more kept changing from green to red, till ten and a half o'clock..."

In Baltimore, the *American and Commercial Advertiser* reported:

> Those who happened to be out late on Thursday night had an opportunity of witnessing another magnificent display of the auroral lights. The phenomenon was very similar to the display on Sunday night, though at times

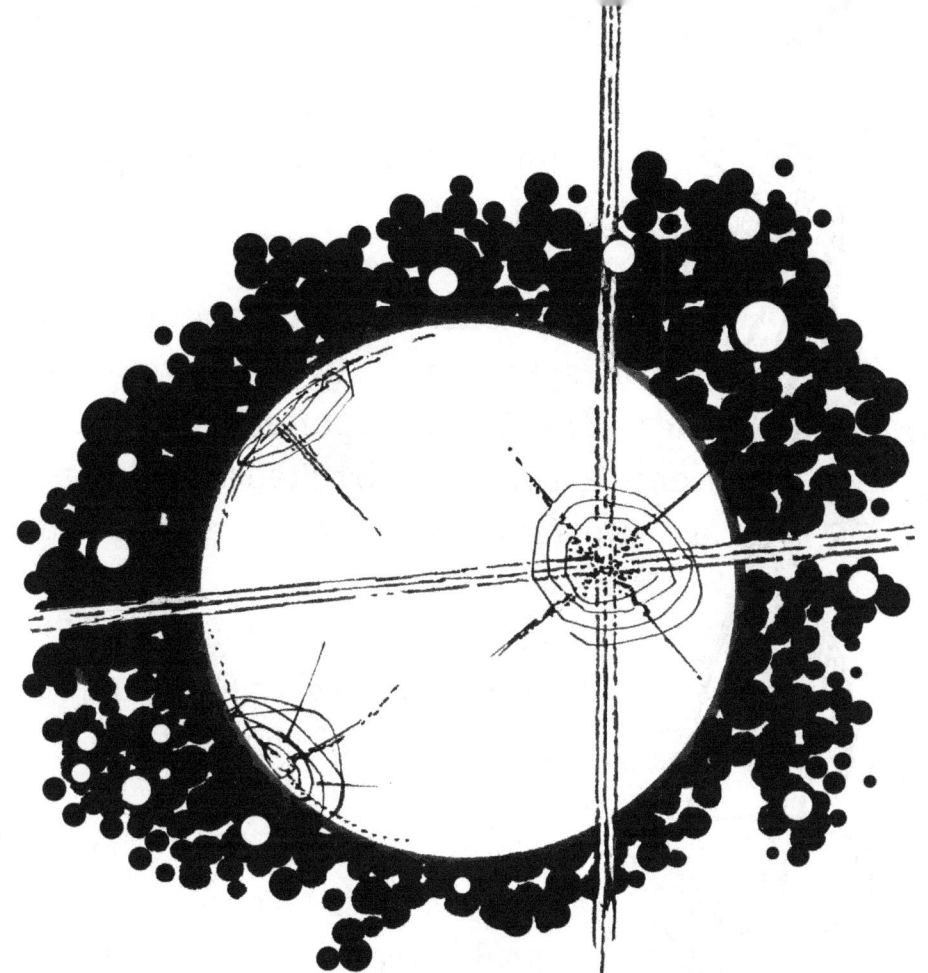

the light was, if possible, more brilliant, and the prismatic hues more varied and gorgeous. The light appeared to cover the whole firmament, apparently like a luminous cloud, through which the stars of the larger magnitude indistinctly shone. The light was greater than that of the moon at its full, but had an indescribable softness and delicacy that

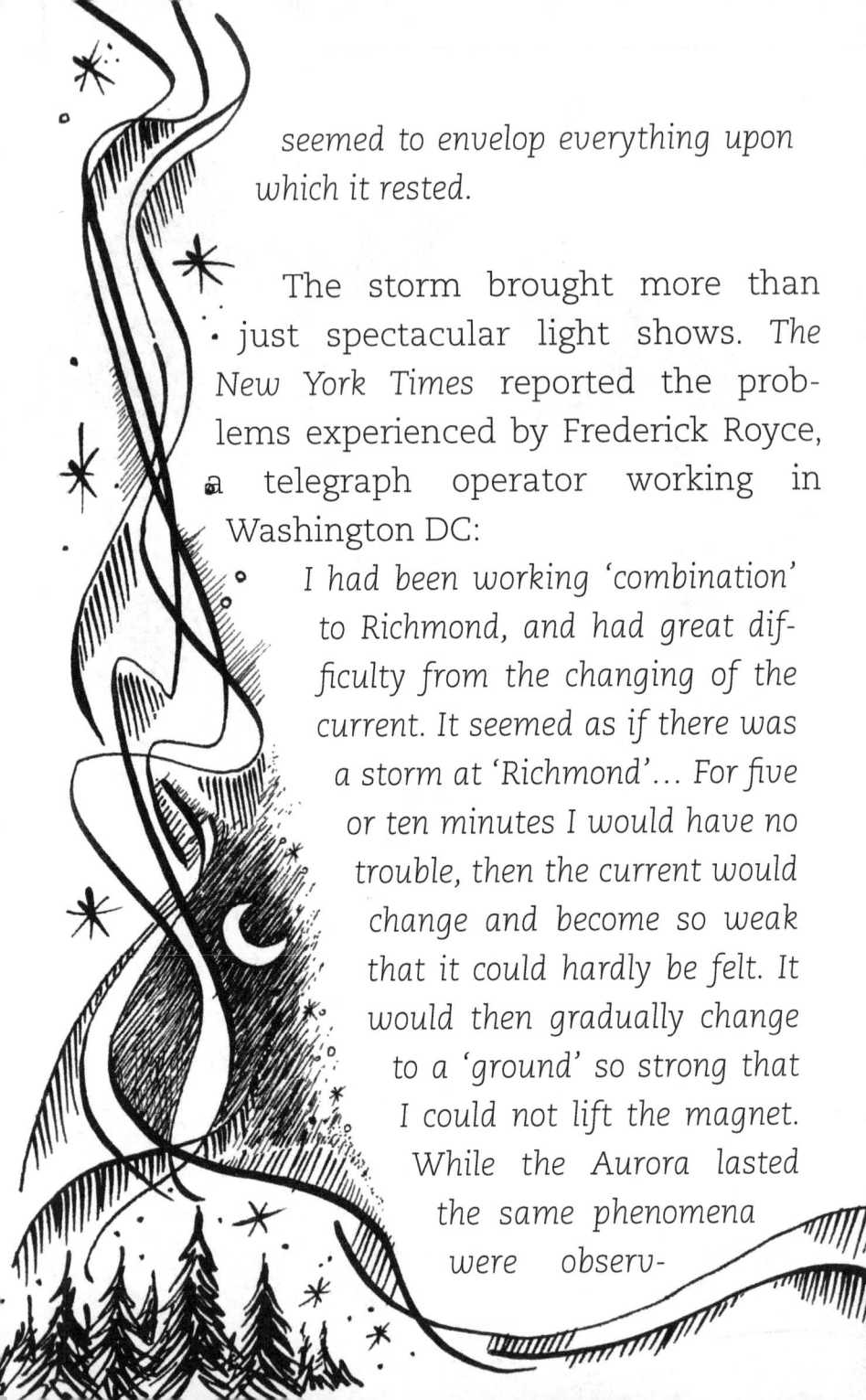

seemed to envelop everything upon which it rested.

The storm brought more than just spectacular light shows. *The New York Times* reported the problems experienced by Frederick Royce, a telegraph operator working in Washington DC:

> I had been working 'combination' to Richmond, and had great difficulty from the changing of the current. It seemed as if there was a storm at 'Richmond'… For five or ten minutes I would have no trouble, then the current would change and become so weak that it could hardly be felt. It would then gradually change to a 'ground' so strong that I could not lift the magnet. While the Aurora lasted the same phenomena were observ-

able... The Aurora disappeared a little after 10 o'clock – after which we had no difficulty, and we worked through to New York.

During the display I was calling Richmond, and had one hand on the iron plate. Happening to lean towards the sounder, which is against the wall, my forehead grazed a ground-wire which runs down the wall near the sounder. Immediately, I received a very severe electric shock, which stunned me for an instant. An old man who was sitting facing me, and but a few feet distant, said that he saw a spark of fire jump from my forehead to the sounder. The Morse line experienced the same difficulty in working.

The *New Orleans Daily Picayune* reported more mundane problems:

The influence of the Aurora Borealis has been felt in the Garden District. We see in the police reports, this morning, that several denizens of that delightful spot have been found drunk— many under a strange delusion, having taken the gutter for their own comfortable beds.

Fortunately, the storm occurred before the electric grid had become such an important part of everyday life. Researchers at Lloyd's of London estimate that if a similar storm happened today, power on the East Coast could be out for up to a year. And, the cost from the damage could easily be more than a trillion dollars.

Thought Question

How do you think your life might be affected if the electrical system went down for days? For weeks? For months?

_____
_____
_____
_____
_____
_____
_____

FASCINATING 5 FACTS
YOU MAY NOT KNOW

1. During the Carrington Event, some machines continued to work for a while, even after the power went out.

2. According to physical evidence, the Carrington Event was probably the largest solar storm in the last 500 years, but smaller solar flares happen multiple times a day.

3. In the event of a large solar flare, astronauts in space can survive as long as they are inside their spacecraft.

4. One solar flare can give off more energy than a million nuclear bombs or millions of volcanoes.

5. Solar flares are hot—they can be more than 3 million degrees Fahrenheit.

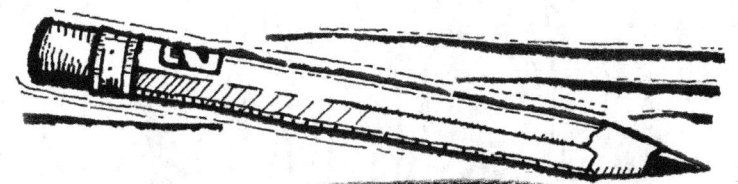

WORD SEARCH

```
M N Y H C A R R I N G T O N K
Q D T B A I K Y Y K K M X B L
V T P D A U K G V R F U X B S
H K G P A A T S Z P H B P N C
H T E D X H P I T K A N N B W
K C O H S T C B E O B B E C I
R Z M P M R S H L P R Y E A K
A O A F S P R Z E U R M L G L
L C G U A N E D G U E R E Z M
O Q N C R A U R R A L H C O G
S Y E H C O B S A V G Y T G K
U M T E R M R J P L I S R O V
N M I A O X R A H C F K I E D
Q L C E W R Z C V N J W C B G
S V E W M J F S O Y X D Q Z F
```

AURORA	CARRINGTON	ELECTRIC
FLARE	GEOMAGNETIC	SHOCK
SOLAR	SPACE	STORM
SUN	SUNSPOT	TELEGRAPH

OCTOBER 8, 1871

The Midwest Goes Up in Flames

October started out unusually hot and dry. The summer had been a drought in the Midwest. The booming lumber industry hadn't always bothered to burn away the brush they cleared. Sparks from passing trains could ignite small fires. With the long drought, small wildfires had become just another part of life in the region.

When a massive cold front hit on October 8, 1871, strong winds fanned the flames across Wisconsin, Northern Illinois, and Michigan. Suddenly all the little wildfires were connected into an immense firestorm, large enough to sustain its own wind system and even generate tornadoes.

The fires in Michigan claimed over 1,000 lives. But the worst fires were in Wisconsin. A local minister, Reverend Peter Pernin, described the chaos:

> The air was no longer fit to breathe, full as it was of sand, dust, ashes, cinders, sparks, smoke, and fire. It was almost impossible to keep one's eyes unclosed, to distinguish the road, or to recognize people, though the way was crowded with pedestrians, as well as vehicles crossing and crashing against each other in the general flight. Some were hastening towards the river, others from it,

whilst all were struggling alike in the grasp of the hurricane. A thousand discordant deafening noises rose on the air together. The neighing of horses, falling of chimneys, crashing of uprooted trees, roaring and whistling of the wind, crackling of fire as it ran with lightning-like rapidity from house to house—all sounds were there save that of human voice. People seemed stricken dumb by terror. They jostled each other without exchanging look, word, or counsel. The silence of the tomb reigned among the living; nature alone lifted up its voice and spoke.

The Peshtigo Fire covered an area about twice the size of Rhode Island. It claimed twelve rural communities before burning itself out. Well over a thousand people in the frontier town of Peshtigo perished on October 8. Some were victims of the fire itself.

Some died from drowning or succumbing to hypothermia while taking refuge in the frigid water of the river. *The Great Chicago Fire* remains the most famous fire of that day. But the firestorm known as the Great Peshtigo Fire was the most lethal.

Thought Question

Why do you think the Great Chicago Fire gets so much more attention than the Peshtigo Fire, when the size and number of casualities was so much lower?

_____

_____

_____

_____

_____

_____

FASCINATING 5 FACTS YOU MAY NOT KNOW

1. Most wildfires are started by humans, but can also be caused by lightning, volcanoes, and extreme heat.

2. Large wildfires affect the weather around them, even causing tornadoes, sometimes called "firenadoes."

3. Millions of acres of land are burned in wildfires every year in the US alone.

4. Fire can obviously be destructive, but throughout history people have used controlled fires to improve the land for farming.

5. The Camp Fire in California in 2018 was the worst U.S. wildfire in 100 years, with more than 80 deaths and somewhere between $8-12 billion in damages.

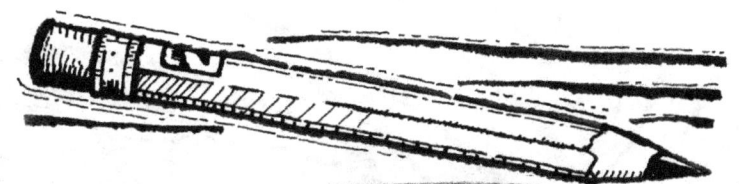

WORD SEARCH

```
J J W W Z I A D M B G G M L F
I L W I I F X K P N L T P X E
J Y W F O L U A K H M B R L N
W V C I Y Y D J Z L T F H O Z
X D J R R P V F A N E G Y X O
C N T E X S U H I X M F Y E N
W A I S S C T H A R P Y R J I
P F N T E E T A E H E C L Q S
X N H O L W O X F N R S K E N
P M H R F K D D N L A D U R O
Y L B M U I J I A D T R P C C
H L Z T E Z F A M N U M U Z S
D E U Q L W M L N L R I V D I
P D T S U D W A S I E O A C W
A O G I T H S E P D X R T K P
```

FIRESTORM	FUEL	HEAT
LETHAL	MIDWEST	OXYGEN
PESHTIGO	SAWDUST	TEMPERATURE
TORNADOES	WILDFIRES	WISCONSIN

AUGUST 21, 1883

The Mayo Clinic is Conceived in an F5 Tornado

The day was beautiful and clear as Drs. Will and Charlie Mayo visited their patients in Rochester, Minnesota. But later it became stiflingly hot and humid and an oppressive haze covered the city. At 6:00 P.M. the brothers drove their buggy to a slaughterhouse on the north side of town. They wanted to procure a sheep's head on which they could practice eye surgery. As the buggy made its way, the brothers kept an eye on the sky.

Arriving at the slaughterhouse, they found the workers leaving early, and they were warned to take cover. Fleecy clouds scudded rapidly across the sky. The dark mass in the west took on an evil greenish cast. Rain came down in sheets, the heavens blazed with lightning, and a massive funnel cloud bore down with a terrifying roar.

Just as the Mayo brothers took refuge in a blacksmith's shop, its roof was torn away. The roof of the Chicago & Northwestern depot was also torn off and the roundhouse demolished. The railroad bridge was blown into the river and the Broadway Bridge was destroyed. Cole's stone mill was blown in. Eight railcars were overturned and two carloads of flour dumped. The spire of the Lutheran church was blown off. Gilman's factory was demolished, the Rochester Harvester Works were ruined, Whitten's warehouse was destroyed, and the County Courthouse and the high school were wrecked. The water had been sucked right out of Cascade Creek, leaving fish beached on its banks. Livestock and buggies and debris were scattered and strewn everywhere.

Mayor Samuel Whitten telegraphed the Governor: "Rochester is in ruins. Twenty-four people are killed. Over 40 are seriously injured. One-third of the city laid waste. We need immediate help." That night the mayor organized volunteers to begin rescue efforts. Townspeople pulled the dead from flattened homes. They rushed the injured to Rommel Hall, a dance hall transformed into an emergency hospital.

The two Mayo brothers, their brother-in-law Dr. David Berkman, and their father Dr. William Worrall Mayo took charge of the trauma ward. The senior Dr. Mayo quickly realized that the task of caring for patients around the clock would require more helpers. He called on Mother Alfred and the

Sisters of Saint Francis, teachers at the local Catholic school, to tend to the patients. The Sisters responded and nursed the patients until the temporary hospital closed.

After the storm, Mother Alfred recognized that the growing city of Rochester needed a full-time hospital. She proposed that the Mayos could be the resident physicians and the Sisters of St. Francis would provide nursing care. The Mayos were not sure. They thought the town was too small to support such an ambitious venture, but Mother Alfred insisted. The Sisters proceeded to raise all of the money needed to begin.

Once Rochester was best known for its wheat. Today it is world-famous as the home of the Mayo Clinic.

Thought Question

Why do you think some people become stormchasers? Would you like to get close to a tornado? Why or why not?

_____

_____

_____

_____

_____

_____

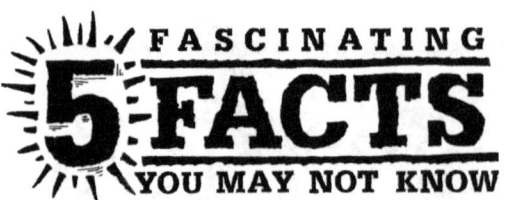

FASCINATING 5 FACTS YOU MAY NOT KNOW

1. The great tornado was actually a series of three tornadoes in the same area, which caused about $700,000 (almost $18 million in 2020 dollars!) in damage.

2. You might think that tornadoes happen mostly in the Midwest, but they occur in every state in the United States, and on almost every continent in the world!

3. In the northern half of the world, tornadoes generally rotate counter-clockwise, but in the south, they move clockwise. But occasionally the same storm might spawn tornadoes that rotate in opposite directions.

4. In an F5 tornado, winds are estimated to be more the 260 miles per hour, which is fast enough to lift houses and cars off the ground and throw them in the air!

5. About 1,300 people were killed in Bangladesh in 1989 in the worst tornado in history.

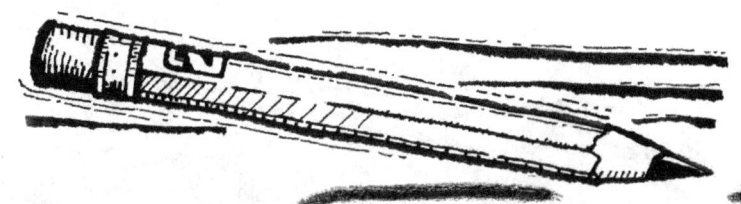

WORD SEARCH

```
X C Q H P O P L Z Y J X R Y R
M R O T S R E D N U H T E D T
T E M T O R N A D O M R P V I
Z Z E J E M M L S R E T S I S
V C U C R L B X U E H P D R V
B S Y B E O A N T W V K E E Y
N R A L S P C T I F S K B F T
X E Z U L E M H I F C W R U M
F H Q X T M O A E P H Y I G G
S T M Q N V K M I S S V S E I
Z O N Y D K S C V X T O Y A M
K R A T O S E N N I M E H M I
X B E M E R G E N C Y K R A V
T P A O H T X S G X G Q M N M
U U C L I N I C J T W V T G G
```

BROTHERS CLINIC DEBRIS
EMERGENCY HOSPITAL MAYO
MINNESOTA REFUGE ROCHESTER
SISTERS THUNDERSTORM TORNADO

MARCH 12, 1888

The Blizzard of '88

It seemed that spring was finally on its way to Boston. The winter had been very mild and weather had warmed up nicely for several days. Crocuses were starting to pop up in the Public Garden. On the evening of March 11, 1888, a gentle rain began to fall. Then it started to pour. By early the next morning the rain turned to snow. It proceeded to snow more and more heavily. By evening, whiteout conditions brought life to a standstill in Boston, and monster waves battered the coastline.

The storm stalled off Rhode Island, and a blizzard raged across New England, as it continued to snow and snow and snow. For four days it snowed. Fifty inches of snow fell in Connecticut and Massachusetts and forty inches covered New York and New Jersey. The hurricane force winds blew the snow into drifts up to fifty feet high. The snow reached the second floor of many buildings. In some places only chimneys were visible.

As the winds blew and the snow fell, the temperatures dropped into the single digits. Men and women with factory jobs tried desperately to make it to work so that they wouldn't miss out on their wages. In North Adams, a millworker on his way home was found just a short distance from the mill. He was stuck in a drift on Main Street, frozen to death. The local newspaper reported that the wind was so loud that it drowned out his cries for help.

Men living in the suburbs took the streetcar to work in the morning, but the trip home was a life-and-death struggle. The rapid accumulation of snow and drifts immobilized railroad cars. Passengers and crewmen were stranded without food, water, or heat. Passengers trapped in stranded railroad cars burned the seats and other wooden components to stave off the cold. Telegraph poles snapped under the force of the wind and snow. The headline "CUT OFF!" appeared on front pages. Horse-drawn omnibuses and streetcars were quickly abandoned in the drifting snow. Snowplows drawn by teams of horses tried to clear the main streets, only to block the side streets and sidewalks. People were found a week later in snowdrifts. Two hundred ships were grounded, and at least 100 sailors died. Fires broke out, but the fire stations were immobilized.

All told, the storm was responsible for as many as 400 deaths along the East Coast. It took weeks to recover. Soon afterwards both Boston and New York began serious discussions about moving their public transit underground.

Thought Question

Do you think it would be easier or harder to survive a massive snowstorm like this today? Why?

_____

_____

_____

_____

_____

_____

1. People were not the only casualities of the Great Blizzard—farm animals and wild animals also died by the thousands.

2. One result of the Great Blizzard was the development of underground utilities and underground transportation systems, like subways, in big cities like New York and Boston.

3. In 1972, in Iran, a blizzard dropped up to 26 feet of snow and caused the deaths of more than 4,000 people, the most ever.

4. A blizzard is more than just snow—it must also have winds of more than 35 miles per hour.

5. If you get stuck in a blizzard, don't eat the snow—try to keep moving, keep covered, and keep dry!

WORD SEARCH

```
Y  W  B  U  Y  C  C  O  Q  P  V  C  Z  Y  O
T  Y  O  J  U  N  C  O  A  S  T  L  I  N  E
Y  O  J  X  N  B  V  L  B  F  Y  R  F  C  J
C  F  O  V  D  D  L  X  S  Y  Q  I  W  R  U
W  O  N  S  E  V  M  D  T  F  C  M  Y  W  X
G  C  Z  S  R  D  N  H  R  S  V  M  D  H  T
D  N  A  L  G  N  E  W  E  N  F  O  E  I  K
Z  L  U  D  R  I  Z  V  E  O  L  B  P  T  Y
T  O  F  R  O  W  O  W  T  W  N  I  P  E  K
C  U  T  P  U  E  R  K  C  P  A  L  A  O  U
W  I  P  D  N  H  F  D  A  L  C  I  R  U  H
L  W  C  E  D  D  L  L  R  O  B  Z  T  T  A
B  L  I  Z  Z  A  R  D  M  W  O  E  K  X  M
H  X  G  V  M  W  M  L  M  S  H  D  J  E  J
H  G  G  S  Q  S  B  Y  O  H  J  P  N  K  X
```

BLIZZARD	COAST LINE	FROZEN
IMMOBILIZED	NEW ENGLAND	SNOW
SNOW PLOWS	STREET CAR	TRAPPED
UNDERGROUND	WHITEOUT	WIND

MAY 31, 1889

The Great Johnstown Flood

It had been a night of heavy rain. Elias Unger, the president of Pennsylvania's South Fork Fishing and Hunting Club, walked out of his home. He went to inspect the dam which held back the waters of his club's three-mile long lake, Lake Conemaugh. The South Fork Dam was notoriously leaky. He was alarmed to find the waters on the verge of overwhelming it.

Unger rallied a crew to try to relieve the pressure on the dam by cutting spill-

ways. But the water kept cresting over the top of the dam and washing parts away. Fearful for their safety, Unger ordered his men off the eroding dam. An hour and a half later the dam collapsed, and 20 million tons of water barreled downstream.

The torrent plowed through the town of South Fork and the village of Mineral Point. It picked up houses, trees, debris, and momentum along the way. At just after four in the afternoon, the inhabitants of the city of Johnstown heard a low rumble that grew to a "roar like thunder."

Boiling with huge chunks of debris, the wall of floodwater grew to sixty feet high. It tore downhill at forty miles per hour, leveling everything in its path. Thousands of people desperately tried to escape the wave. Instead they found themselves swept up in a torrent of oily, muddy water, surrounded by tons of grinding debris.

The mountain of debris piled against the Pennsylvania Railroad's Stone Bridge. Then it caught fire. Dozens of people who had managed to cling to floating bits of houses were

swept directly into a deadly inferno. When the floodwaters finally receded, 2,209 people had died. It was the deadliest single disaster in the United States at the time.

Thought Question

Why do you think people write songs, make movies, and build museums to commemorate destructive natural disasters like this?

_____

_____

_____

_____

_____

_____

_____

FASCINATING 5 FACTS YOU MAY NOT KNOW

1. The Great Johnstown Flood was not a total surprise because the dam had broken before and engineers had warned that it might happen again.

2. The story of the flood was depicted in a 1926 movie, a 1940s Mighty Mouse cartoon, and several songs and poems.

3. Flash flooding can occur with no warning and can cause other problems, like mudslides.

4. Less than a foot of water can be enough to knock a person over, and just a few feet of flooding can cause serious problems, like your car or truck floating away down the street.

5. One of the major dangers of floods is the lack of clean, safe drinking water afterwards.

WORD SEARCH

```
Q V T Z R B C O N E M A U G H
G N D E R H M E W A P F W K L
F P V K F T F X E J O L E L R
P I E A T N E R R O T A H J W
R V R L H J T U N F F S J Q K
D Z R E X S K K W C G H G R Y
K I M Z N N R V I M K F L K U
B Q J W W Y X J R C N L Q G F
I I O U D A O M G E M O S D E
L D U E R O S I O N X O U N C
T P J P Z M K M S E E D Q U R
L M A O U G A X M O U Z D T O
C A O F W X X F D E B R I S A
T D P C W O A D T E X P E V R
C P D R S P I L L W A Y S H I
```

CONEMAUGH DAM DEBRIS
DOWNSTREAM EROSION FIRE
FLASHFLOOD LAKE RIVER
ROAR SPILLWAYS TORRENT

MARCH 25, 1911

The Triangle Shirtwaist Fire

Lena Yaller was 19 years old and sewed on the 9th floor:

My dressing room was near the elevator near Washington Place, so as soon as I took my pocketbook I had heard a girl holler "Fire!." I wanted to turn my face so then I seen this girl- you know, she was a very jolly girl. She used to like very much to fool us, often saying "Here comes the boss," "Here comes the floorlady"—and there was nothing. So when I turned my face and I saw she is the one, why than I didn't pay any attention to her afterwards. Just continued my work in the dressing room.

When I got near the dressing room, then smoke was coming up all around us, in my face and in all the windows, up by all the windows, so I wanted to run my face back. I saw flames coming up from the Greene Street side. I wanted to turn around to Greene Street, so instead of going to Greene Street the girls were crowded around that place waiting for the Washington elevator, because I seen all the girls were out at that Washington Place. They pushed me into the dressing room, so I could not see anything else. It got very dark and I felt a draft so I wanted to go out, so I seen some breezes coming out from someplace, so I wanted to make my way over to see where it came from. I seen it came from the Greene Street window.

Near the Greene Street it was a window and there is was near the elevator, so I wanted to and made my way through the door I wanted. As soon as I pass I seen the examining tables were all burning. As I was passing by I seen smoke. You can see everything burning and I seen the rest of the girls remained in the dressing room, so when I passes the window I opened the window. The window, I saw, opened down, so I wanted to open the window. It opened double, and opened out, and so I burned my knee from the steam heat, so I turned back and stood there about two or three minutes. Of course it seemed more than four hours from me, but I knocked at the elevator that it should come up, and I seen—I turned my face and I seen the door was burning from the elevator—the door was burning from the doors, that door was burning in the factory, so I wanted to jump out of the roof, to go upstairs on the roof, so I burned my arm, my head, my hair and all, but I went on the roof and then some fellows from the Washington Place took me out together on the roof.... All the people what I left in the dressing room are all dead....

Thought Question

What precautions do you have at school in case of a fire? What do you have at home? Who should be responsible for fire safety in these locations?

_____

_____

_____

_____

_____

_____

_____

FASCINATING 5 FACTS YOU MAY NOT KNOW

1. In less than twenty minutes, workers at the Triangle Factory died from jumping out of the building, falling down the elevator shaft, and burning/smoke inhalation.

2. Some of the workers at the Triangle Factory were only teenagers, almost all of them were women, and most were recent immigrants.

3. The rescue efforts were poor because firefighters' ladders and hoses were too short to reach the top floor, doors were locked from the outside, and the fire escape broke quickly.

4. After the fire at Triangle, new laws and regulations were developed around workplace safety and inspections.

5. There are thousands of fires in the workplace in the U.S. each year, and about 100-150 people die from workplace fires or explosions every year.

WORD SEARCH

```
A F I R E E S C A P E Y A T P
V Y V C G F O M W V A P J S T
T A J A L A D D E R S V X N C
Y M S E Y C W I P R W P F O R
S E H O S T Z R V E O S I I X
H J I B T O L U I G Y G R T X
O B R S X R H Z A U Z E E I N
T W T O N Y P X T L C K M D L
M P W X Y Z I T Q A N I G N D
K N A G O Y W E N T D R O O T
O I I C V D H P X I X T C C M
G N S V I I O M A O V S F K N
C Y T E O Y I S O N S L R I G
I M M I G R A N T S D J Q Z W
W G C C M S T I X E L H M X E
```

CONDITIONS   EXITS   FACTORY
FIRE   FIRE ESCAPE   GIRLS
HOSE   IMMIGRANTS   LADDERS
REGULATIONS   SHIRTWAIST   STRIKE

JUNE 22, 1918

The Hammond Circus Train Disaster

There was great anticipation in Hammond, Indiana, the day summer arrived in 1918, during the Great War. The children of the town would be treated to the big arrival of the circus. There would be a parade, and elephants and clowns and lions and tightrope walkers for the crowds to see.

The Hagenbeck-Wallace Circus had visited Hammond before. Now it was coming back for a fifth visit to present its fabulous spectacle in the Show Grounds on Calumet Avenue. Advance press agents and bill posters had plastered the town. This premier circus would arrive on three special trains. Its roustabouts would set up twenty-two tents for its 400 performers. It promised to be the most spectacular show ever seen in Indiana.

Just before dawn, at about 4:00 A.M., the train had to make a stop near Ivanhoe in order to cool an overheated wheel bearing box. The brakeman alerted the conductor with a signal flare to signal the engineer to bring the train to a halt. Red lights were turned on to warn any other approaching trains that a train had stopped on the tracks.

Meanwhile, an empty Michigan Central troop train was barreling along at full speed along the same tracks. It was piloted by an engineer who had previously been fired for sleeping on the job. He ignored the red lights, two automatic signals, and the frantic signals of a flagman. The train plowed into the

caboose and four rear wooden sleeping cars of the circus train.

Upon impact, the circus train's kerosene lamps ignited its wooden passenger cars. A massive fireball erupted. Eighty-six people died. Many were roustabouts who were known only by nicknames: "Baldy" and "Smiley" and "4 Horse Driver." Also dead were the "Great Dierckx Brothers" strong man act; Jennie Ward Todd of "The Flying Wards"; Verna Connor, a Wild West rider; her husband, James, who was in charge of the horses; the McDhu Sisters, another equestrian act; Zeb Cattanach, the circus's lighting rigger, and his wife, Bessie; and Joe Coyle Jr., two years old, billed as "the youngest clown in the United States."

The Hagenbeck-Wallace Circus borrowed acts from Ringling Brothers and Barnum and Bailey and other circuses. The survivors of the disaster bravely put on the next scheduled show at Beloit, Michigan.

Five days after the crash, the survivors gathered to bury their dead. The Showmen's League of America had just bought a sizable plot of land at Woodlawn Cemetery in Forest Park, Illinois. They could scarcely imagine how soon it would be needed. The coffins arrived on three trucks. 1,500 mourners, most of them circus people, gathered to pay their last respects.

According to circus lore, if an elephant's trunk is up, it's a sign of joy or triumph. A lowered trunk is a sign the animal is mourning. The "Showman's Rest" memorial is marked by five granite elephants, their trunks lowered in mourning. They keep watch over the large plot maintained by the Showmen's League in Woodlawn Cemetery.

Thought Question

Trains were still relatively new at the time of this accident. High-speed and mag-lev trains are today's newest innvoations. Would you be concerned about traveling on new technology? Or would you be excited? What about even more extreme modes of transport, like space rockets?

_____

_____

_____

_____

_____

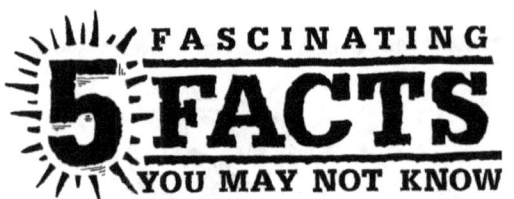
FASCINATING 5 FACTS YOU MAY NOT KNOW

1. The Hagenbeck Wallace Circus had already suffered two train crashes, killing over thirty-five people, and a flood near the Wabash river, which washed away many of the circus's animals.

2. It's really hard for trains to stop suddenly—it can take over a mile for modern trains to come to a complete stop.

3. The elephant statues at the cemetery were rumored to mark the spot where five circus elephants died during the train accident, but the circus animals were not actually on this train.

4. The deadliest train crash ever was in Sri Lanka in 2004—more than 1,700 people died.

5. Believe it or not, there are more than 5,000 train crashes every year in the United States (mostly train-automobile collisions), causing about 600 deaths.

WORD SEARCH

```
D M E C V N L I G W T P Z J E
Q Y I C O N E O M P H X M M H
N Y N W H C Z R S B J G P G P
I P S P D E G B I N D I A N A
A X J J N X S B Z F O G Q S A
R B O Y O Y C O C P F H G H E
T S X W M R Q H O D Y C Q O N
T A P W M I D J S B E X C W E
M M Z C A L Q I M A A C V M S
C L E O H A O D M U R C G E O
R O T C U D N O C N Q C L N R
D I L F Q E L E P H A N T S E
E R A L F P O N A P R R I P K
Q C I R C U S R N C C K L R R
G L U N Z S K U S U O W G S Z
```

CABOOSE   CIRCUS   CONDUCTOR
CRASH   ELEPHANTS   FIRE
FLARE   HAMMOND   INDIANA
KEROSENE   SHOWMEN   TRAIN

SEPTEMBER 2, 1935

Great Labor Day Hurricane Hits the Florida Keys

Ernest Hemingway was at home in Key West when the storm hit. He told what he saw in an article written for the magazine New Masses:

This is the way a storm comes. On Saturday evening at Key West, having finished working, you go out to the porch to have a drink and read the evening paper. The first thing you see in the paper is a storm warning. You know that work is off until it is past and you are angry and upset because you were going well...

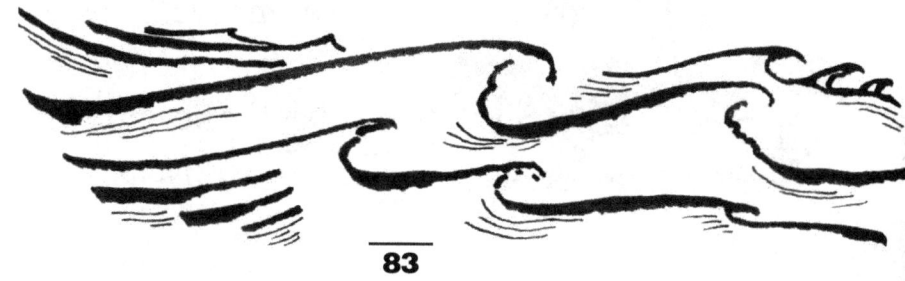

You go down to the boat and wrap the lines with canvas where they will chafe when the surge starts, and believe that she has a good chance to ride it out if it comes from any direction but the northwest where the opening of the sub-basin is; provided no other boat smashes into you and sinks you. There is a booze boat seized by the Coast Guard tied next to you and you notice her stern lines are only tied to ringbolts in the stern, and you start belly-aching about that...

The wind is bad and you have to crouch over to make headway against it. You figure if we get the hurricane from there you will lose the boat and you never will have enough money to get another. You feel like hell.

But a little after two o'clock it backs into the west and by the law of circular storms you know the storm has passed over the Keys above us. Now the boat is well-sheltered by the sea wall and the breakwater and at five o'clock the glass having been steady for an hour, you get back to the house. As you make your way in without a light you find a tree is down across the walk and a strange empty look in the front yard shows the big old sappodillo tree is down too. You turn in.

The eye of the hurricane passed. Papa (as Hemingway was known) was able to ride out the storm. To the east however, on the low-lying, unsheltered islands of the Florida Keys, a thousand World War I veterans had been building a road as a part of the Public Works for Veterans program. They never had a chance. When he got there, this is what Hemingway saw:

The railroad embankment was gone and the men who had cowered behind it and finally, when the water came, clung to the rails, were all gone with it. You could find them face down and face up in the mangroves. The biggest bunch of the dead were in the tangled, always green but now brown, mangroves behind the tank cars and the water towers. They hung on there, in shelter, until the wind and the rising water carried them away....

Camp Five was where eight survived out of 187, but we only find sixty-seven of those plus two more along the fill makes sixty-nine. But all the rest are in the mangroves. It doesn't take a bird dog to locate them. On the other hand, there are no buzzards. Absolutely no buzzards. How's that? Would you believe it? The wind killed all the buzzards and all the big winged birds like pelicans too. You can find them in the grass that's washed along the fill. Hey, there's another one. He's got low shoes, put him down, man, looks about sixty, low shoes, copper-riveted overalls, blue percale shirt without

collar, storm jacket, by Jesus that's the thing to wear, nothing in his pockets. Turn him over. Face tumefied beyond recognition. Hell he don't look like a veteran. He's too old. He's got grey hair. You'll have grey hair yourself this time next week. And across his back there was a great big blister as wide as his back and all ready to burst where his storm jacket had slipped down. Turn him over again. Sure he's a veteran. I know him. What's he got low shoes on for then? Maybe he made some money shooting craps and bought them. You don't know that guy. You can't tell him now. I know him, he hasn't got any thumb. That's how I know him. The land crabs ate his thumb. You think you know everybody. Well you waited a long time to get sick, brother. Sixty-seven of them and you got sick at the sixty-eighth.

And so you walk the fill, where there is any

fill and now it's calm and clear and blue and almost the way it is when the millionaires come down in the winter except for the sandflies, the mosquitoes and the smell of the dead that always smell the same in all countries that you go to—and now they smell like that in your own country. Or is it just that dead soldiers smell the same no matter what their nationality or who sends them to die?

Thought Question

Imagine you knew nothing about hurricanes. What would you think the first time you saw one?

_____

_____

_____

_____

_____

_____

FASCINATING 5 FACTS
YOU MAY NOT KNOW

1. A train was sent to evacuate the veteran workers, but it was too late—the train was hit by the storm and the cars were thrown off the tracks.

2. No one predicted the 1935 hurricane would be so strong.

3. When the storm and storm surge made landfall, all the clocks nearby reportedly stopped at the same time.

4. The 1935 Hurricane was one of only three Category 5 hurricanes (wind speeds over 150 miles per hour) to hit the United States in the last 100 years.

5. Hurricanes have been reported as long ago as when Christopher Columbus arrived in the Caribbean, and have been responsible for more than 2 million deaths.

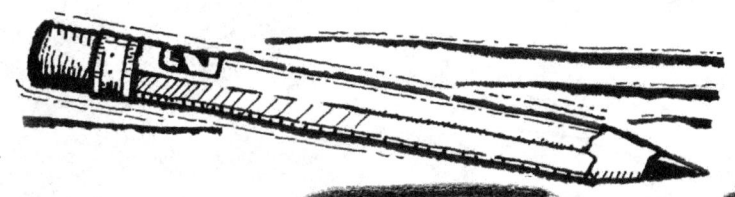

WORD SEARCH

```
H R H G M F Q X U L Y P G S D
H O B F O P X T U P G Y M K C
B P K Q C S S U R G E Q F E P
M L Y S K C O L C X G G L Y R
H U R R I C A N E B I S O S O
C M I O T R A I N B C N R F A
B P S P O V Z V L G J E I A D
H N L L A F D N A L J H D W S
W W E V I F Y R O G E T A C Y
B Y A W G N I M E H N A K N W
R L E Z X G W F E H Z Z A O D
E Z D S K V G Y U F W F K A L
V R O S H F L H S M L L B C K
J S K R O W C I L B U P S A F
P L Z W P E H S N A R E T E V
```

CATEGORY FIVE
HEMINGWAY
LANDFALL
SURGE
CLOCKS
HURRICANE
PUBLIC WORKS
TRAIN
FLORIDA
KEYS
ROADS
VETERANS

AUGUST 18, 1961

"The Birds" Invade Santa Cruz

"**S**EABIRD INVASION HITS COASTAL HOMES; THOUSANDS OF BIRDS FLOUNDERING IN STREETS" read the headline in the *Santa Cruz Sentinel*.

A massive flight of sooty shearwaters, fresh from a feast of anchovies, collided with shoreside structures from Pleasure Point to Rio del Mar during the night. Residents, especially in the Pleasure Point and Capitola area were awakened about 3 a.m. today by the rain of birds, slamming against their homes. Dead, and stunned seabirds littered the streets and roads in the foggy, early dawn. Startled by the invasion, residents rushed out on their lawns with flashlights, then rushed back inside, as the birds flew toward their light.... When the light of day made the area visible, residents found the streets covered with birds. The birds disgorged bits of fish and fish skeletons over the streets and lawns and housetops, leaving an overpowering fishy stench.

The most learned explanation of the bird tragedy came this morning from Ward Russell, museum zoologist at the University of California. He said the shearwaters generally live in the southern hemisphere. As far as they are concerned this is their winter flocking area. Often when they are disturbed while feeding they will rise in flocks from the water. A blinding fog covered the coast last night and this morning. "They probably became confused and lost and

headed for the light," he said. The only light available was the street lights and overnight lights in some homes and businesses.... Russell said that this is a fairly rare phenomena and it takes certain atmospheric conditions to cause this confusion. He said that during very foggy conditions the lighthouses along the coast are struck by the thousands of seabirds.

Famous film producer Afred Hitchcock lived nearby. He reportedly saw this strange news. He called the *Sentinel* for more details. Hitchcock was already working on a film adaptation of Daphne du Maurier's story "The Birds." There are a lot of similarities between the real-life story in California and her short story. Daphne du Maurier's story was set in England. But it also involves seabirds attacking a small town. These strange events in California may have inspired or influenced Hitchcock. Yet few people are aware that the famous movie had some basis in reality.

Thought Question

What would you think if an enormous flock of birds suddenly appeared all over your town and stayed? Would you feel differently about a huge number of frogs? Snakes? Squirrels? Why or why not?

_____

_____

_____

_____

_____

_____

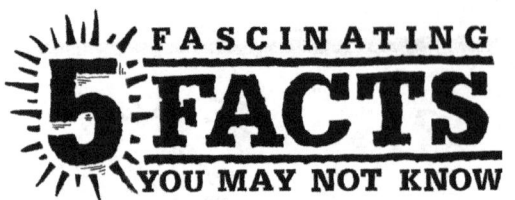

5 FASCINATING FACTS YOU MAY NOT KNOW

1. It turns out that the birds that "invaded" California in this real-life story were not confused by the weather—they were poisoned by a toxin found in some algae blooms.

2. In 1991 in Monterey Bay, California seabirds died in large numbers again, probably from the same toxic algae.

3. In other weird bird news, millions of blackbirds suddenly appeared in Scotland Neck, North Carolina, in 1969, making many birds and people sick (from bacteria in their droppings) before they disappeared again.

4. In 2013, a huge influx of birds came suddenly to Hopkinsville, Kentucky, where people used air cannons and other noisemakers to try to scare them away.

5. Tourists still "flock" to Bodega Bay, California, to see the sites where the Hitchcock movie was filmed.

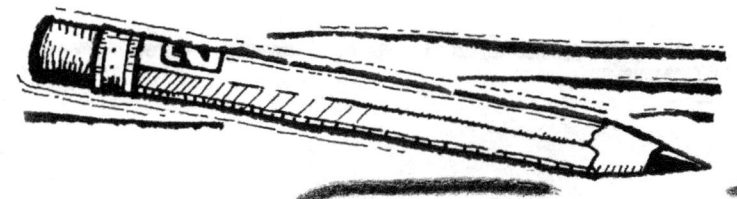

WORD SEARCH

```
L E H S R E T A W R A E H S W
D E D I L L O C I J O H S K L
G D J V B H R T R S L F X F Z
T D B T R B U Y R T L O O C S
G F U S I T I D O S U G O C R
B W B R H W G I Q I E J A O E
X T D N P X C C Z R P V X N K
F S U R L N B A Z U Z P D F A
H I T C H C O C K O R A F U M
E E L P J X H I Y T C M W S E
T V Y M U V G O J A L G A E S
J R G W S E B M Z U S F E D I
N K O F Y L F O P A Y R O F O
U D E Q V U U D Q P I Z H L N
S N I X O T Q V B L M C B E N
```

ALGAE
CONFUSED
FOG
SHEARWATERS
BIRDS
DOMOIC ACID
HITCHCOCK
TOURISTS
COLLIDED
FILM
NOISEMAKERS
TOXIN

Word Search Answer Keys

T	D	M	Z	N	A	E	B	B	I	R	A	C	N	E	
D	U	H	A	Q	M	N	O	I	G	Y	H	L	W	W	
G	S	C	U	R	A	A	H	T	W	S	E	F	B	H	
L	Y	G	A	Z	T	C	U	K	E	D	Y	H	A	N	
A	G	A	J	B	N	I	B	S	H	I	P	S	M	E	
M	F	M	E	E	A	R	N	S	R	G	N	I	W	U	
T	Y	P	R	L	A	R	B	I	R	R	B	T	W	K	
Q	B	F	C	R	R	U	B	I	Q	Y	I	I	Q	I	**Page 7**
I	U	I	K	O	P	H	W	A	W	U	N	R	H	F	
I	Q	P	M	N	Z	D	I	J	D	D	E	B	C	R	
S	G	F	N	B	G	C	R	E	S	O	Y	C	V	N	
S	Y	L	T	K	U	E	S	Y	O	Q	S	J	U	W	
R	L	X	Y	L	S	E	I	N	O	L	O	C	D	O	
H	K	K	T	I	F	M	W	P	P	F	V	B	F	R	
O	I	S	R	N	O	I	T	U	L	O	V	E	R	D	

Page 15

P	I	X	L	B	Z	N	U	Q	T	J	K	C	A	X
R	Z	Y	M	I	B	E	P	X	H	I	E	D	X	E
E	O	O	X	I	V	W	A	Y	U	B	H	S	Z	C
D	F	Y	O	P	A	M	S	G	N	G	R	I	N	M
I	D	N	E	F	P	A	O	N	D	F	C	R	I	D
C	Z	B	L	A	O	D	G	M	E	F	R	U	N	C
T	M	F	Q	X	R	R	G	P	R	I	J	O	U	Y
I	P	P	I	S	S	I	S	S	I	M	N	S	P	I
K	O	O	P	C	X	D	A	R	K	N	E	S	S	Q
D	S	Q	S	H	A	K	I	N	G	N	Z	I	M	O
E	K	A	U	Q	H	T	R	A	E	V	K	M	Z	F
G	S	S	N	D	R	N	W	H	Z	C	L	M	P	I
T	G	V	B	D	S	V	D	I	A	N	Y	M	K	S
V	D	C	G	C	L	Z	Y	Y	R	O	R	R	E	T
P	W	P	G	C	U	R	R	E	N	T	L	U	F	F

101

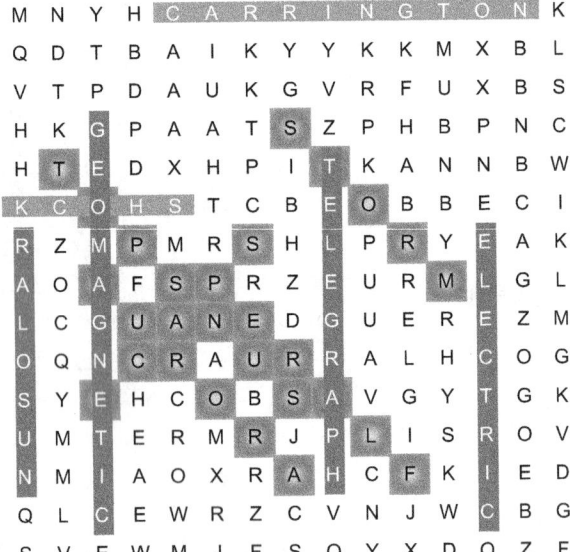

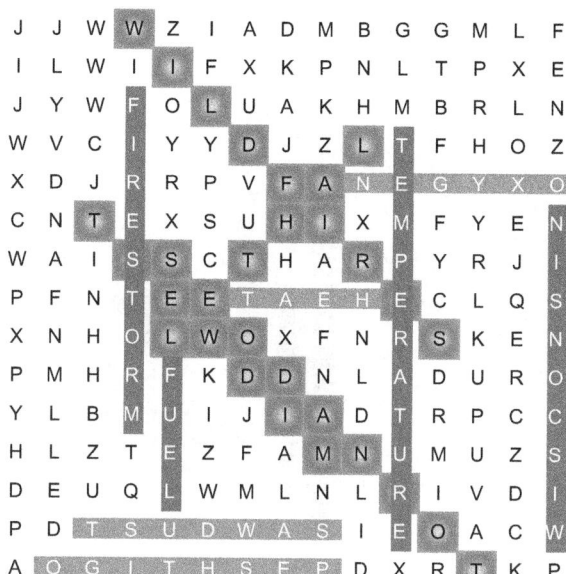

Page 41

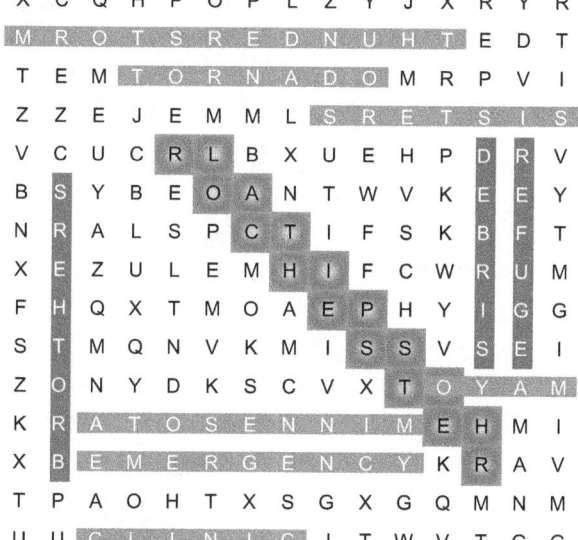

Page 49

103

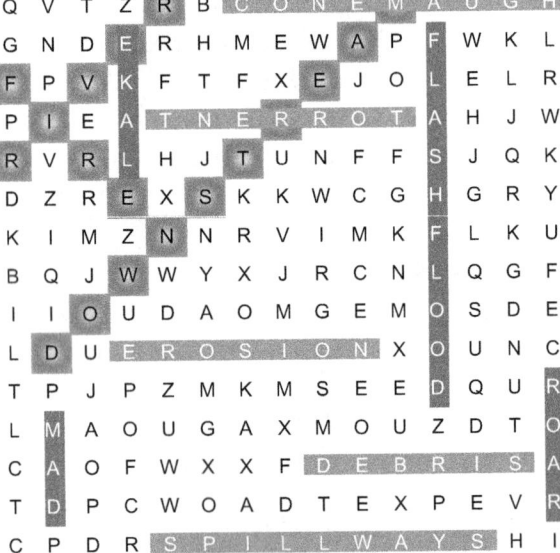

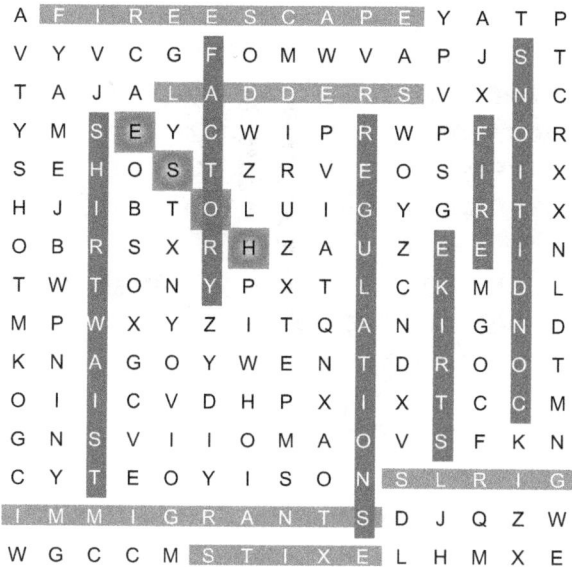

Page 73

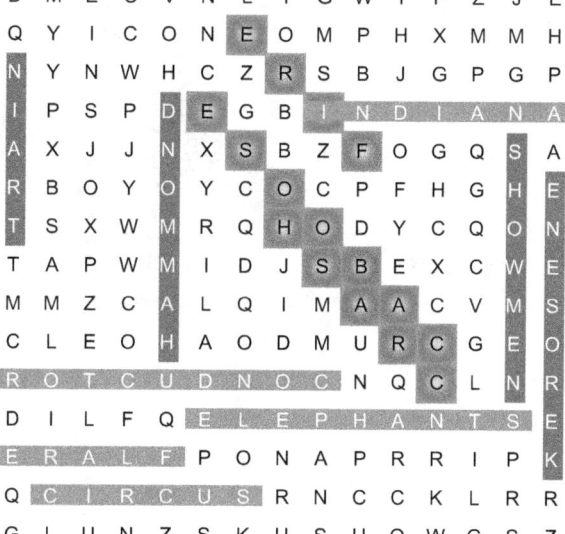

Page 81

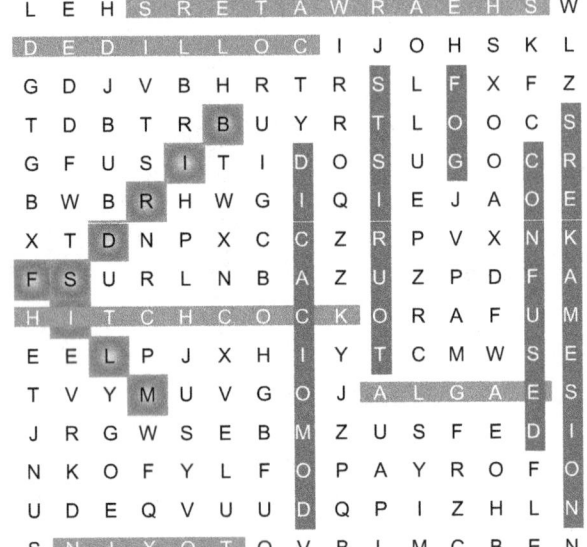

CPSIA information can be obtained
at www.ICGtesting.com
Printed in the USA
LVHW080023140720
660556LV00003B/22